Papilio

Carol Phelan Aebby

ISBN: 978-81-934055-8-1

First Edition: 2018
$21 / Rs. 200/-

Rochak Publishing
HIG 45 Kaushambi Kunj, Kalindipuram
Allahabad - 211011 (U.P.) India
http://www.cyberwit.net
Tel: +(91) 9415091004 +(91) (532) 2552257
E-mail: info@cyberwit.net

Printed at Repro India Limited.

Author's Note

I write to inspire thoughts on beauty and humanity; to stimulate union and cerebration on free thinking and justice; and to witness my time on this planet Earth.

There is no greater muse to my Soul than the butterfly. She visits my dreams, lands in my wombs of thought and inspires my heart to see what the eyes cannot see; and to hear what the ears cannot hear; and to feel what the flesh cannot feel. She inspires me to spread my wings through life, open my heart through strife; and pick up my pen when I feel something miraculous within. Butterflies symbolize each eternity, womanhood and love. They reside within our souls and fly through our eternity bringing sweetness and beauty that cannot be owned. So this book I have named, **"Papilio".** Each story is like a wild flower kissed gently by a butterfly residing between the reality of earthly life and the unseen greater existence that watches over and embraces our daily lives.

Contents

A Woman's Heart

A Woman's heart is made up of sensitive
Edifying engines, and compartments...
Each one with its own mystery and secrets,
Waiting to be touched to create wonders.

It can happen in a fleeting magic moment,
And endures for the rest of her life;
— Or serve as a pillar of emotions —
Helping her to live lightly and lovingly!

A woman's heart is the central dynamo
That energizes the engine of creation,
And fuels the wings intuition and dreams!

Quality Time

nt of justice I live...
eats to pump wonders and life
— In the reality of my days; —
On the trail of wisdom to the path
Of freedom, where life is shared, and grace
Abounds in quality time of love...

I feel your embrace from deep within;
The warmth of your presence strengthens my will;
Courageous I course the path of justice,
— Edifying my mind, soul and heart —
With mellific bricks of love and fairness,
Free with you in harmonious time!

All of our lives lived made us of today
To co-create wonders, to understand
All boughs of the Human Race's tree...
So I keep the course forward to new sights
With constructing thoughts of beauty, smiling
To live a quality life with you!

The Drinker

There he sat, sitting on a stool, cradling his whiskey in his trembling hands. His shoulders drooped over holding all the problems of the world. I had watched as he entered the bar, a charismatic smile on his handsome face as he took the first drink to his lips his charm had oozed with grace. Confidence had returned with finely brewed hard liquor into an environment he liked to call sublime space. The bartender seemed to be a familiar face and they chatted amicably for a few hours. Learned he was, an entertainment to all, as he quoted from poets and books with a natural flair and a mind of greatness. Then all went dark...

The bar was full of faces, saliva drooling from dead lips, souls that had taken their craving for alcohol to their deathbeds. I sat in a corner and watched as they pushed into his body and clung to him from outside. He could feel the weight as he slipped into his abyss. He had drunk too much and I knew that this could be his last. I swooped over to him as the glass touched his trembling lips. I could hear voices...cold and taunting:

"Drink it...drink it... drink it..."

He looked at me...

A bright light engulfed him, miserable souls fled from him to a corner of the bar. He gently lowered the glass full of whiskey and looked at it in puzzlement. I embraced him and led him out of the bar into the fresh crisp night. He took a deep breath and cried tears of joy, tears of hope and tears of relief.

"Who are you?" I heard him say "I know someone is here. I can feel your presence."

I jumped inside him. His soul was black no more, but his heart and mind were burdened by life. I came out and stayed with him as he started home.

Without words I said to him:

"Sweet man and sensitive soul, do not burden yourself with Earthly matters. You do not need more than enough to live. Love is the currency of life not gold."

"I know someone is here, and I hear you. Strange as it seems, I feel you like a gentle electric current through my being. How could I have put down that last whiskey? How mysterious that my craving was gone! Thank you, my friend, please come back again."

As we reached his house, a young boy no more than seven was sitting on a step watching.

"Sean! What are you doing up? You should be in bed."

"Dad, I was waiting for you. I wanted to help put you to bed."

"Son, blessed child of mine, your Dad has quit. This will be the last night on this step for you."

"Yes, yes, Dad... Come on... let's go to bed."

"Have I ever told you that you are the best son a man could ever have?"

"Yes Dad, many times."

"I quit! No more whiskey, this is the truth."

"Yes Dad... no more whiskey!"

The boy put his arm around his father and led him into the house. Little did he know that what his father had said was true. I did not want to go and could have stayed to watch this tender love grow...

But my duty waits...

The Visitor

Sitting on bed in her living room she was
As still as a propped up human corpse!
Her beautiful hands resting on her lap;
Eyes glazed over; I jumped inside her pounding
Heart; the turmoil unbearable so still outside,
Yet tempestuous! It was my first time
To witness a crying heart; and paralyzed soul.

Hours before I saw her, laughing and joking
With her children as she sent them off to school.
I was in her reality; — a dark place to be, —
Foreboding and lost... I moved out, and sat nearby...

Suddenly she said, "Who are you? I know someone
is here I can feel your presence." Silence reigned...
"Thank you," she whispered, "Whoever or whatever
you are, welcome." She smiled sweetly. "I don't know
what is wrong with me; I don't sleep nor eat.
When I do, doze off for every such a short time;
I dream of past lives, furry spiders and cobwebs.
I cannot talk to anyone, for who would listen?
How would I explain the depth of my despair?
But I can feel you here a helper of sorts."

Suddenly her face brightened... "I know who you are.
My inspiration." With that she grabbed her pen,
And started to write. The words flowed like melting
Gold from pen to paper. On her beautiful face,
There was a special light around it... Then she said:
"I must be crazy talking to the air. How long will you stay?
Please, stay; don't ever leave me, for this despair
terrifies me. I want to die, but I cannot;
I want to live, but I cannot; the only peace
that soothes my mind is the release of words from pen
to paper. My heart lightens, and my torment fades
for just a little while; but now I know you are here
with me... understanding what no other human can."

Silence was broken... "Thank you; I know you must go
now. I believe that there is more beyond
my knowledge of this world, an unseen universe.
I ask only one thing, please come back often,
I will always know when you are near. Thank you."

I embraced this sensitive soul with light.
She felt the warmth, and smiled sublimely.
The fire had been rekindled; the torment,
And fumes of black smoke, released from her
As I absorbed the torment, and hug her again!

I stayed with her for the most part of the day,
Accompanying her on to work and to school
To pick up her children; and talking constantly
Of her derangement. I answered her questions
To the air, and she could hear me without
Any language. I left her with her children... reluctantly,
For there is an overpowering attraction
To an enlightened soul; it is mellific...
Sweeter than the most delicious chocolate
In the world... Warmer than the loveliest embrace;
And happier than the first smile of an infant.
I will be back my love... — whispering softly; —
And with that I left her human world behind...

The Waitress

There are many faces in the crowd rushing to places indifferently. Persecuted expressions reign on Earth today. Going to work has lost its appeal since a coming home has become unreal. I walk into a café on a corner and take a seat. There is one waitress being worked off her feet. She looks so defeated and is causing customers to curse her for the terrible mistake of mixing orders, due to her over load of tasks to accomplish at the same time. She is exhausted and confused to sour the cream on a blueberry tart. One customer can take no more and stands up screaming, ferociously cursing her! The boss comes out all apologies and gives her a look to behave herself or else...

This is the breaking point of this I am sure; she grabs a knife from the chef and holds it to her throat. A silence blankets the café as tears roll down her face. Not a word does she say, with a look of a trapped animal for this is it! What could possibly have happened to this young woman to make her wish for death? I jump inside her tormented soul as blackness engulfs my every move. Into her mind I flow with speed and see the abuse that she has received. Her children now at home one sick, another refused to go to school and her spouse, lifeless, in shock after losing his job sits on the sofa in silence.

I embrace her soul as black plumes release into the café with relief as I spread my arms absorbing them into me. She drops the knife and passes out as some warm hearts run to her aid. While unconscious she lies, I fly into her mind.

"Who are you?" she asks, "Is this a dream, I can feel something sweet. Are you an angel?" Then she continues... "Thank you, I feel light and strange, a relief somehow. I reached a breaking point, didn't I?"

I answered her without a word.

"You are an angel, of that I'm sure, please don't leave me. Such a lovely sensation... What should I do? ...Yes, you are right! I am priority number one, I am a woman..."

She giggles.

"I haven't laughed in oh so long... my heart closed to all. My children need me, my man needs help, I work and work, but cannot pay the bills... clawing my way through life each day without a break. Fear stops me... you know... fear that if I stand up for myself, I will lose the only job I have and then we will starve."

I answer her...

"Sweet Jenna, you are beautiful, you are a precious mother, strong and mighty you can stand any storm. Show the world what a Goddess you are!"

With that her eyes opened to concerned faces.

"Get her some water... give her some air..."

Jenna sat up with a smile on her face, a sparkle never seen before, how pretty she looked a deep confidence within. She waited on tables for the rest of the day with love and a spring in her step. In the evening she sat with her boss and discussed a better arrangement.

I accompanied her home. She stopped at a cake shop and bought four cream puffs. With cake box in hand she skipped her way home and burst into her house with a cheery grin. The children ran into her open arms happy for the mood she was in, and her husband sat at the kitchen table as they indulged in their little treat. The children's chatter she listened to, hugging them often and giggling too. A little spark she did see in her man for sure, as he pulled her onto his lap and kissed her cheek.

Do not doubt a swift change for it can happen in a day, a moment in time when a heart is opened and love streams in.

"Jenna, my love, how is your heart today?"

"Open, my darling, open... it is all I can say!"

I want to stay, I always do but I have to move on to the next.

The Moon and You

There is such a beautiful moon tonight.
I was looking at it, thinking of you,
Then I thought on the beauty of hers,
And the wondrous moments you bring
Into my life; — the reality that I know; —
As my heart pumps Grace flowing Love
Through my flesh, and alimenting my Soul;
I feel you, understanding our completion
— The giving receiving the synergy —
Of union in the magic of togetherness
In a castle of devotion that we call home.

I look at the moon again and see you...
A thought lights up: "Loneliness is lack of Love."
So I thank heavens for your constancy;
For knowing what to say, and for expressing it
When wisdom dictates how to guide your voice...
For recognizing your Love in me
In all of your lifetimes as my inspiration,
Always fueling the wings of my Soul;
And for coloring my dreams with hues
From the rainbow of affinity and creation;
And for keeping me in the light of your smile!

On The Edge

A terrifying vision I did receive, and with speed, I arrived on time to prevent a horrific scene. A girl stood on the edge of a cliff in a remote place. I did see her walking through the wood; her step slow but steady, however all her senses had shut down. I followed her as she reached her destination, the fatal ledge. She stood balancing on the edge, too far into her abyss for me to enter. Emotions were dead only one purpose in her mind: that of death. She leaned forward looking down. I embraced her pulling her back. With a bewildered look she straightened up and walked back to the edge raising her foot to take a step into death. I embraced her once again and pulled her back. Undeterred, she shook her body and walked back onto the ledge, with more determination than before. I swiftly embraced her and pulled her back once more. Then she opened her mouth and screamed to the heavens:

"If I want to die, I have a right to be allowed to die. This is my life!"

Then she fell to the ground.

It was now so dark; a sound of an owl and some crickets were all that we could hear. A cool breeze caressed her cheeks. She was coming out, just a few more steps up and I would be able to enter. She picked herself up from the ground once again, wavering slightly she walked back to the ledge. I waited as she leaned forward, outstretching my arms ready to pull her back, when she suddenly swung around and looked through me.

"Who are you?" she said 'I know I am not alone."

I saw a tear in her eye and gave a sigh jumping inside her. Her soul was being strangled by black plumes, I engulfed them with light and they released to the outside; and without a moment to lose I absorbed them...

Katie fell to the ground tears streaming curled up in a fetus position, rocking to and from. I did not say a word, put my arms around her and held her all night in the wood without another soul in sight.

Helios arrived all smiles, and a new day was born. Katie did not wake so warm was she in my Light embrace.

"Katie! Katie!"

Many voices I did hear coming closer and closer... then she was spotted.

"Katie! Thanks heavens!" her father said with tears streaming down his face.

He picked her up...

"My sweet heart, don't you know how much you are loved? If you were to die, our world would die with you!"

"I'm sorry Papa." Katie whispered, and then one more time louder "I'm sorry!" as she sobbed into his shoulder.

I watched silently from the side. Suddenly she stopped crying and looked at me.

"Thank you, my angel, for my life!"

I believe that it is impossible to see me, but maybe she did.

"Katie, you are so beautiful... walk forward and face life with love, courage and wisdom." I said

"I will." she answered.

"Who are you talking to, love?" Her father asked.

Katie smiled sweetly and said... "My heart, my soul, my mind and my flesh..."

It was time for me to go, but I will always watch over her soul.

Pond of Soul

Pond of soul stillness waits
Hidden secrets on timeline plans,
Lost in thought of loves long gone,
Wishing for hope and a new dawn!

Happiness revives dreams of youth
Of lives gone by and retreat,
Kissing swollen eyelids as tears flee
Lulling the heart to a blissful new...

Chambers of the heart hold pains of past
Laughter; smiles and love too...
A plea, a cry, an answer sweet;
A womb of love, justice and peace!

Ana sat by the pond of her soul in stillness beyond any thought. Lost and grieving for all that had gone. Her eyes rested on a little stream —trickling out of the pond slowly — downhill. Little tears involuntarily fleeing a body of pain to return to the earth again.

Still it was...

Not a sound being permitted entry into the chambers of a broken heart. Ana felt a tickling on her palm and without thought raised it to her lips, replacing it gently onto her lap. She had not been aware of her action. Then, the tickling returned. Again she raised her palm to her lips, kissing its restlessness and replacing it on her lap. A tear spilled down her cheek slowly, quietly dropping onto the back of her hand. Ana didn't notice. She hadn't seen the sun rise, or the sun set for a few mornings. She had been submerged in a state of nothingness. Time had stopped. Then, she heard a beautiful voice steal quietly into her silence:

"Ana... come back..."

Ana did not move.

"Ana... look..."

Ana raised her eyes slowly. Thousands of butterflies were dancing around the pond. Her eyes started following one to the other. Then children's giggles gradually seeped into her ears. They were playing hide and seek. Ana felt a pop in her heart as the pieces started floating towards each other.

Can you see me?

Ana looked to her right: A beautiful lady was sitting beside her. Her hand was on Ana's and she was smiling. Ana could see sunflowers blossoming in her eyes.

"Look into the pond..."

Ana said, "I can't..." Her heart was aching, her breasts were swollen, and her stomach was tied up in sadness. If she was to see any further, the emotions could bring an unbearable pain.

"Trust me — look into the pond — of your soul."

Ana looked in, and she saw her many lifetimes; her loves, her friends, her children and off spring, her hurts, her sorrows, her bliss and her survival.

"You do not grieve the end of one part of your soul plan; you embrace it and move on. Yes, it becomes a part of you. You do not give up. You do not slow your heart beat into a forced departure. You love it, cherish it, look at the canvas and take the first step forward."

Ana felt a tingling throughout her being; a warmth void of heat, a love void of conditions, a tear void of sadness, and her face broke into a smile. Her heart started beating energetically. Helios caught her with his rays and swept her into the skies with a rich laughter. He tossed her to Selene and she kissed her on the cheek. Ana spread her wings flying from star to star, dancing with joy on clouds of wondrous thoughts through her wombs of peace; justice and love to the child of her heart, returning to the pond of her soul, ready to light up the world.

Ana squeezed her companion's hand.

"What do you believe with all your heart and soul...? You have always believed this and it has helped you through so many storms."

Ana thought for a moment, and...

I believe that real love does not hurt; it nourishes the heart, soul, mind and flesh. It resides in each blade of grass, butterfly, flower, plant, tree, stream, ocean, mountain, star, the sun, and the moon. It holds life together in its warm embrace; and it never fails to create wonders.

"My love, you are back! And true love is the love I have for you. So keep your pen flowing, your heart glowing; and fight for justice, truth and peace."

Ana woke up in bed, her pillow soaked in tears. Helios on her face and life kissing her lips!

An End to Abuse

I heard the humming before seeing the little girl sitting on a step in front of her house. She had a doll in her arms and was rocking it to sleep.

"Hello Denise! How are you today?"

"I'm great, Mr. Flynn." she answered her neighbor with a smile that could melt a thousand angels and one.

Then she looked at me...

"Hello." she said

I looked behind me to see if we were alone. She can see me... how wonderful!

"May I sit down little lady?"

"Yes," she said smiling courteously.

She continued to hum her lullaby until she was sure that her doll was asleep. Then she whispered...

"Who are you?"

"Didn't you call me, Denise?"

"Are you an angel?"

"Yes, I am."

"Please stay with me."

"Denise! Come and set the table, your father will be home soon;" her mother called out from inside the house.

Her little body stiffened and her breathing became short.

"Sweetheart, don't worry, I am here. Now, let's see what is happening in your home. "She stood up and walked into an extremely clean and tidy house. I followed her into the kitchen to where her mother was at.

"Mama, Mama! I have an angel."

"That's marvelous, sweetheart, hurry up and set the table. If I do it for you Papa will give us a hard time. So let's hurry."

I sat down in a corner watching the two. Denise's mother was beautiful, soft and sweet. Her hair was caught up at the nape of her neck and she was wearing a blue and yellow dress. The perfect family it would seem, but I knew that that was not so.

They stopped in their tracks as the sound of Papa's car came to a halt in the driveway.

Denise, it's Papa. You'd better go out and say hello or he will be in a bad mood all night.

I followed Denise outside.

"Hello Papa!" Shyly she said.

"How's my little girl?" said Papa as he got out of the car. He held his arms open and she walked into them for a hug. Then hand in hand they walked into the house.

"Denise!"

"Yes, Papa."

"What's your doll doing on the floor of the entrance?"

"I'm sorry, Papa, I forgot to bring her with me."

She grabbed her doll and ran to her room with it.

Denise's mother had come to the entrance with a smile on her face.

"How was your day?" she said.

"Fine, we had good business..."

He continued on and on following her into the kitchen. I noticed that he had not enquired about her day; in fact he had shown no affection towards her. Denise returned and started to help her mother.

"How about a beer?" asked Papa.

"Yes, just a minute..." Mama said as she took a beer from the fridge.

Then she went to get some nuts. The color drained from her face as she stood in front of the cupboard.

"I'm sorry; we seem to be out of nuts."

Denise dropped the plate she was holding... her mother ran to tidy it up.

"Mama, I'm sorry."

"Don't worry sweetheart, it is only a plate. Did you hurt yourself?"

"What do you mean...no nuts...?"

"I'm sorry, I thought we had more. I can go out and get some."

"No! It's ok."

Denise and her mother looked at each other and I felt a terrible foreboding.

I stayed patiently in the corner of the kitchen until they sat down to the dinner table.

"Denise, straighten your back!"

"Yes Papa."

"What way is that to hold your knife and fork. Hold them properly."

"Yes Papa."

Silence reigned as they began to eat.

"This is too salty, I can't eat this!" Papa's voice broke into the silence like an ice-pick.

"Really? I think it is alright."

"What did you say?" he glared into Denise's mother's eyes.

Denise physically seemed to get smaller and I knew that I must protect her.

I whispered in her ear.

"Denise, let's go to the toilet."

She understood and said...

"May I go to the toilet please?"

"Of course honey." Her mother answered as she fidgeted with her napkin.

I led Denise to her room and told her to stay put. Then I arranged some angel music as she picked up her doll and lay down on the bed.

I rushed back to the dining room...

Denise's father's plate was now on the floor and he was stomping around in the kitchen making some more. Mama was still sitting at the table deep in despair. I jumped inside her. Her whole body was trembling, plumes of black smoke had engulfed her soul, her mind had been paralyzed and her heart was fearful. I jumped out as the black plumes released to a corner of the room. Then I opened my arms and absorbed them.

"Who are you?" She whispered. "I know someone's here."

"I have been in your mind; I have seen the abuse you have endured. For your sake and your daughter's you must stand up to him and walk out this evening before he realizes what is happening. Do not bring anything, just you and your daughter."

"How can I do that? He has isolated me from my family and friends. I have no one to ask for help."

"When you stand strong and see the woman within, when you put yourself first and let love in, then an army will help you. Trust, this is the moment, this is the day."

A calm expression came over her face... a silent confidence gave birth within... She stood up and walked into the kitchen. He was feverishly preparing food for himself.

"We are over." she said.

"I know! He replied, and as she turned to walk away he shouted after her. "And you'd better get a job for I won't support you anymore!"

Denise's mother put the car keys in her pocket and went to Denise's room. She had fallen asleep. Taking her daughter in her arms she walked out into the street. When they were both in the car, she turned on the engine and drove and drove... no tears, just a calm she had not known in years.

After an hour, Denise's mother found herself on the steps of an old friend's house. Her friend saw her from the window and came running out.

"May we stay with you for a short while?" Mama asked.

Her friend threw her arms around the two, as tears streaming down her face.

"Of course, my darling, it pleases my heart to have your company. Let's call your family and our friends; we will all help you to get through this. The light in your tunnel is shining bright!"

I did not leave that night. As Denise's mother and her friend drank tea and chatted, I held Denise in a Light embrace. Next morning, when she awoke, I whispered...

"Denise, do not fear any more... all has been cleared. Your Mama left Papa and Granny is coming today."

"I love you, my angel. Please don't go!"

"I must, my sweet, but I will come back often, and if you ever need me again, I will listen."

With that she fell asleep again.

I stood watching the two of them and slowly moved on...

Butterfly on my Window Sill

Butterfly on my window sill...
Look how pretty you are, so still,
Magenta and gold, pink and brown;
A master design of nature
In the window, you do wander...
Land on my table, no wonder,
Pretty! Welcome to my abode!
Paused in purpose I gaze and sigh
On to my quill a sudden perch...
Now this is magical... special,
How gentle you are, trusting friend,
Perhaps this could soon be your end!
With a smile, I gently stand up
Quill held, butterfly unperturbed,
Back to windowsill I do stroll...
Thank, you inspirational muse.
It is a sweet moment like this
That triggers the heart to true bliss;
Enhances the soul with enchantment,
And sets the mind to precious thought!

Stroll with an Artist

In colors unique hues solitary thoughts flow...
— All vibrates alive in heart and soul's emotions —
Depicting on canvas a nightmare of past blues;
A stroll under Helios' smile is a gift of life!

Magical hands... beautiful in creation's glow...
Stained with oils, painting the visions of mind in action,
Carrying life's lines in all that one does for art;
Protecting, caring and feeling the touch of beauty.

Old oak standing wise, — its natural wonders shows —
Embracing young lovers; — under its boughs all goes...
Souls entwine, — hearts in sublime time pump spirit's grace,
Reflecting complexity's passion of the moment!

Canvas raised as raindrops abound, — but it's done; —
Paints wet, dripping, mingling with my tears of despair.
Light all-embracing — as soul takes hold in elation, —
Whilst an exoteric masterpiece is conceived!

I looked down at my hands, paint stained. How precious the hands are! How many people know the power of their hands?

These priceless hands of mine can paint hearts, play music, cook a gourmet meal, catch someone before they fall, caress, touch and write.

I study the shape, the length of the fingers, the bone structure, and the lines on the palms; and today the paint splashed across showing the passion of my morning, now abandoned in my studio to take this walk by the river under

Before Helios' gaze and Nature's splendor I smiled to myself, knowing that the nuances of all I wish to depict are here in front of me; caressing my eyes with their lights and shades, hues and fluid strokes. I sat down on a bench, closing my eyes and let in the sounds of birds singing, bees buzzing, children playing; and a voice of a girl talking to her lover.

"You ask too much of me... you truly do! I should not have to prove it to you."

I opened my eyes and saw the young couple sitting under an oak tree. The wise old tree and I touched souls as I glanced down on the scene that I now behold. The girl's head was tilted slightly, and her jaw bone, softly demure teased a brush. Her hands on her lap, — all fingers entwined in each other — fidgeted nervously. Her lips were peach, and Helios, obviously attracted had given them light. The young man was leaning against the bark of the tree looking unperturbed.

"My love, you have to choose him or me. If you choose him, I will be happy to turn my back and walk away. For your happiness is all I live for!"

"How can I choose? I love you both!"

"It is not possible to love two. You can only love one!"

"No! You are wrong. I love you both enough to die for..."

"Then you do not know what love is?"

"You say I don't know love? You are dark and he is light! And you are passionate, he is compassionate; you talk too much; he only talks when it is necessary; — you are an artist and he is an artist; and you are both pure; — and I quite simply love you both! Yes, oh sweetheart! Say what you wish, I love you both!"

Suddenly the young man sat back, now looking slightly concerned.

"You are confused, you are mine. You have always been mine for many lifetimes. We are fated to be together. I can touch your soul like no other. Listen to me! All else is deceit, what we have is real."

"If I was to lose him, I would cease to exist. He holds me in his embrace at all times. I can feel him now. He never asks anything of me, he lives only for me. How can you be so selfish?"

"Selfish? I believe that you are trying to drive me crazy. I am not an egotist. He is an impostor! I am your true love... me!"

I shifted uncomfortably on my bench for this conversation was so intense. There is a whole unseen world of souls meeting, greeting and becoming entwined. Visual it is not, but real it is. That is what I had been trying to portray on my canvas. There is Earthly love for one, worldly love for all, and soul love that can be as complicated as the secrets of the Universe, yet... if heart is open, — and soul is free — simple, it can truly be!

The oak embracing this couple knew all the answers and looked quite amused. We all have one destination and that is to fly back into the embrace of the Light — after realizing that there is only simplicity — for love does not have borders.

I stood up and headed back along my path to the studio. My pace quickened as I ran inside grabbing my canvas. Then I rushed back outside the door as I held it up to the sky silently screaming with all my might. Helios dived behind a cloud as raindrops fell on my work of art. Paint colors of reds and blues now trickling from canvas to hands, elbows, my face, down my neck between my breasts mingling with my tears. I sat down on the wet grass with my canvas running my fingers through my hair in frustration. Then I heard a gentle voice in my head like a sigh parting a storm:

"What is happening here? Bring the canvas inside take a shower and freshen up!"

I stood up doing as I had been told. I put the canvas back on its easel and took a shower.

The warm water cascaded down on me as I watched colors of ponderings flow down the drain. I wrapped myself in a towel and poured myself a glass of water. I took another look at the canvas, ruined for sure, I thought. What smiled back at me was a reflection of all I had perceived on this morning. A true masterpiece... a work of Art!

Golden Notes

Worlds apart, souls entwined; Chopin's notes
Caress hearts speaking of wondrous visions
Of beauty, love, life's drama and peace!

A young lady in the audience sits
— Enthralled, heart open, and mind aware —
As the music seeps her mind to strike
Past secrets to mingle with the present!

Awareness courses her inner brain,
— As notes delicately speak to her —
Leading her soul to enchanting dreams,
While my fingers dance with precise touch,
And confidence over the key board...

The opus of a great soul and heart,
— A true sensitive mind in weak body —
With misery and illness, but brilliant
Throughout our days, — inspiring with beauty...
You're a star on constellation Art!

Ah, beloved Chopin, you glow sublimely!

This is another night: concert, orchestra, conductor; and an audience, however here I stand off stage looking down at my hands. I am not focused... my fingers feel clammy! I pull a handkerchief from my pocketbook, and pat them absentmindedly.

"It is a full house today, Madame!" — Someone murmurs beside me.

I hear my name being announced and walk out on stage to applause. I look out on the expectant audience, sit down to the piano and give a nod of readiness to the conductor. The orchestra starts up Chopin's concerto No. 1 Op. 11 — and I sit ready now in professional mode. My heart bursting with love for this music as my soul poised links to the essence of each and every note.

Then I hear a commotion in the audience:

"My love, we are at a concert, this is neither the time nor place!"

I often find that when I am fully focused on my performance, my senses are heightened and I pick up on a variety of happenings in and around me. My fingers are poised and ready.

"But I need to talk now!"

"We can go for a drink later; I really want to listen to this."

"There was a time when concerts were a place to sit, chat, drink and listen. If Mozart could see us all now, dressed in our best, even afraid to sneeze for fear of disturbing someone's take on a note, he would giggle so much at our absurdity!"

"Silence, please!"

I close my eyes and find myself playing beautifully, fingers taking over, soul synchronized. Ah... this is my time to relax. With a whoosh I find myself in the audience watching my fingers play. I am beside the couple I have been drawn to.

"Darling," she whispers. "I have been having these dreams, this constant yearning and pulling in my navel. I feel I must tell you, for I am also hearing voices."

"Sweetheart," he said, "they are only dreams."

"No! There is a whole other world out there. We are just living on the surface of dimensions, universes, and lives!"

"That is it! I have had it! Tomorrow we are going to visit Michael. I believe that you should talk to him as you are obviously slipping from reality!"

"Michael? The psychologist, why would I want to talk to him? Our ideas of reality are different. You, my love, are in a trance; hypnotized by your environment and society. I have stepped out of the box. I see all so clearly now."

This conversation had captured my attention.

"Be quiet, we'll be thrown out! I don't want to talk about this now. Perhaps we can find someone to help you."

"Are you mad? How can anyone help me? You seem to omprehend what I am saying. I have been bestowed with a gift from the Universe; worlds have revealed themselves to me. I can never step back in... and pretend... you know me better than that."

"To be specific and open with you, I don't know you anymore. You act like a stranger... yes, you are odd indeed!"

I sighed, for I could not help myself. I wanted to tell her that to be aware of such a gift is both a blessing and a curse. All is felt more acutely. I could feel her heart racing and calming — as the notes caressed her soul — giving her time to gather her strength, and do what must be done.

Music is not just a mixture of notes put together to make a pleasant sound, it is a part of the language of the universe. It talks to souls, uplifts hearts, and often clears the pollution of the mind. That is for those who listen with hearts and souls open, embracing love; drinking in the varied emotions of play, love, loss, panic, despair, understanding and victory.

I took a look at myself as I played uplifting hearts with my technique and love, knowing that I am but a fulfillment of a mission...

"If you continue to be unable to understand me, I believe that we are over. I am not strange, insane, and psychotic, I am conscious of my feelings and visions, and I know what I know! Don't you see, all problems and worries are so trivial when one realizes the expanse of lives? How many lives have we lived to get to this moment, sitting here listening to one of the greatest composer of all time. Chopin knew, I am sure of it, he could see beyond his life for if he couldn't, he would never have been able to write such wonders. Through all his physical ailments and mental torture these miraculous notes were conceived showing us true beauty."

I smile to myself and return to the piano stool as the final movement climaxes. With a dramatic finale all comes to a close. As silence falls over the hall, a voice in my head I hear: "Next time, could you please be present, for your wandering is very irritating."

Forgive me, Chopin, I smiled, I meant no disrespect. Then I hear him chuckling as the audience break into applause. I stand up, bow graciously and walk off stage.

In my dressing room all are waiting with smiles; my muses, and a bottle of rose champagne with two glasses, one for my beloved who will arrive soon. I sit down on my chair and smile — thinking on tomorrow newspapers' reviews!

Chains of the Mind

Freedom is all I ask for all;
Understanding is all I plead...
Justice, — where are you to act wise
And cut the chain of the outlaws?!

A friend with a gentle ear — did
Listen to my heart's pain, and cheer;
Take my hand, give me an embrace,
For friendship is the flag of peace!

Steering my way through social strata,
— Indifference and their diseases, —
Matters not to manipulators
Of cynical tricks of the system,
But I will not give up on justice!

Decision's made and understood
— As I take control of the helm, —
And set the course of my life's ship,
Keep on navigating, — fearless —
To the "Port of fairness and Justice.

Is it to be trapped a state of mind?

One can be imprisoned in this world, but still host a free mind, which can develop and create opportunities for freedom.

"I am a prisoner in this country!"

I heard the cry of a woman as I sat down next to her in the waiting room of the family's court house.

"Women have no rights. He, the monster that he is, won't let me issue passports to take my children home so that I can rest with my family. Where is the justice in that? I feel like a beaten dog! I am woman, for heaven's sake! Who on this planet has the right to say what I do, where I go... who in this world has the right to prevent me from visiting my country with my children? Obviously he does, cruelty thy name is 'Man'!"

I did not want to listen to this, I did not want to hear the desperation coming from the chair next to mine, but we never want to know, do we?!

Her friend looked at her with concern, nodding and agreeing to the injustice of it all. Yes, "injustice", but — does not justice always defeat evil? — Does not justice protect the innocence of a mother and her children? Yes, for innocence resides within all those trapped, abused, and tortured, both, mentally and physically. These horrors are endured by innocence on a daily basis.

My heart ached for those I am powerless to help. Then like a flash of inspiration, with an inner impulse, my soul answered my plea. Life is what one accepts or chooses to make of it. Justice does prevail, but one has to rise above the ordeal, look down on it — and cast it out like a small kindling fire. To wallow in one's miserable fate is to invite more atrocities. The mind has the power to pull one through. Step out of the box, live real life and let justice take its course in whatever shape or form. When one pushes defeatism, and dark brooding thoughts out, the light on the path of the winner will shine, — and with this comes invisible weapons — laced with determination and trust.

So, move on sweet lady, do not let any human being pull you down, for you are all powerful, you are the key to your new dawn. If injustice is served, kick it aside. Realization, acceptance and trust in justice, is the key to freedom; and lest I forget, the most important ingredient: "Love."

I closed my eyes and with my mind's strength sent my thoughts telepathically to the next chair where she was seated. Suddenly the woman went quiet.

"Jane, are you alright?"

Jane's friend looked concerned by her sudden silence.

"Anne! I understand. I now know what to do, thank you sweet friend for listening to my ranting."

"What is it? What are you going to do?"

"It's so clear. I don't know why I didn't think of it earlier. I suppose these thoughts don't come until the mind is ready to accept them."

"What are you talking about... such riddle, dee, and dee?"

Jane burst into smiles. How pretty she is, I thought. I had taken out my notepad and pen to do my daily scribbles.

"Anne, don't you see? It is all up to me. I have to stand alone and direct my army."

Now Anne was giggling.

"The lawyers, the mediators, my family seem powerless to help me, but I, my sweet, am all powerful. I know exactly what to do, step by step, for justice is waiting on top of it all. The steps are the key. I will take no more nonsense. Let's go! I must call my lawyer. I have a lot of work to do.

Come here you... give me a hug! I love you; you know that, for listening, nodding, and now smiling."

I took a good look at them as they stood up to leave... Jane's eyes met with mine, and we smiled at each other.

May light, courage, wisdom, bliss and peace go with you, I whispered wishfully to their minds.

As they were leaving, I heard Jane saying to Anne:

"Did you see that woman sitting next to me?"

"What woman? There was no one next to you."

"No. You must have seen her; she had a pen and paper. There was something truly wonderful about her. Oh, Anne! Are you sure you didn't see her? She was a woman, a pure woman, — that is the only way I can describe her."

"Mama, Mama!"

I looked up from my writing pad into the eyes of my daughter. They were sparkling!

"Are you finished writing? Can you give me a lift to my friend Sofia's house?"

I looked around, and dazed. I was in my living room. Did I just dream all that? Did I... or did I experience it?

Of course, my darling; let me get the keys.

"Mama, I love you!"

I grinned, — is that because I am driving you to your friend's house?

Bella giggled, and said, "No way! It is because you are an amazing mother!"

You are becoming a refined young lady, I said, and tickled her.

"Thank You Mama, all that I am, I have learned from you." Bella said, giggling.

OK! Let's go.

I picked up the keys, and walked to the door. Then I heard a mellific whisper in my mind very softly:

"I thank you sweet, beautiful lady."

I stopped for a while, smiled, and ran to the car with Bella.

For Human I am...

Stone throwing a hobby for most; accusing,
Hating and vengeance are rife in a world,
— Losing dignity and sense of humanity; —
And blindly ignoring the Human Race!

I am human, — living as a gregarian
Member of the Human Race, — as Nature
In creativity exemplifies,
Through its laws of diversity in union,
In the gregarious circle of life!

Slumbering in my cells of mind and body,
Is a monster never to be released...?
It must be kept leashed to allow peace's flow,
— Liberating endless goodness from me —
With compassion, courage; wisdom and love,
Human virtues of the highest regard!

I live right, under love's light to comply
With the laws of harmony, — as Nature shows, —
Occupying my seconds to complete
Minutes of productive hours to a day,
Once the emulation of Nature's beauty
Is the never end building of the castle
Of life with its sharing of holy wonders!

"Did you hear what he did?"

"Yes, it is horrific! How could anyone do something like that to the poor victims?"

"Let's not think of it anymore, it is too terrible."

"That's easy to say, but very hard to do as I read all the details in the morning newspaper and now I feel as if they inhabit me."

"Mari is in big trouble, the whole town is talking about how irresponsible she was to do something like that. If I were her, I would move to another town for people will never forget."

"Well she was always a little different, — wasn't she?"

I did not intend to listen to this gossip, but I was standing at a bus stop and had no choice. I looked around at the rest of the waiting passengers. All those alone had earphones and were lost in their own musical worlds. I suppose that is one way to cope, I thought.

The sun was bright and I was deeply feeling life as I perceive it; all the colors, the beauty, the mysteries; the innocence and the — horrors that small town cries — to the big city fears of the world's atrocities!

I am human, I thought.

The terrors I hear and see in the media, read in the papers, and sense, make me cry deep in my soul; — and feel like their author, — once I can't prevent them. Yes... all the horrors I see happening now worldwide lead me to think of myself as guilty of active omission.

If I had been raised differently, if I had experienced such atrocities first hand then — who is to say that I would not be a one of the terrible perpetrators and protagonists? I have it in me as all human beings do when they are pushed to the edge of their frail existence.

So, no matter how terrible the action from next door to the world, I have a duty to always — show compassion, and to keep love's thought flowing with wishes and soul, — touch these horrors and help to release them.

With all my heart I try to understand, although sometimes it is a challenge, but with willingness, love and a fighting spirit, I march forward to challenge the world to join the chain of love, compassion; justice and cooperative attitude.

I will keep on marching, albeit I am now standing at the bus stop, one person among billions; one person with choices, one person holding the power of the universe in the palm of her hand.

A small child runs away from her mother, and reached a dangerous spot on the busy street. Her mother screams out in terror trying to grab her... With one step I have her in my arms!

"Thank you!" the mother says. The little child smiles at me and I give her a wink.

"Sweetheart, don't you ever do that again. You must always stay close to your mother. Her mother gently scolds."

"I'm sorry Mama!" the child says as tears stream.

"Don't cry, my love, it's alright. Let's be more careful."

As they embrace the bus pulls up.

A True Love's Found

Alive feeling that cannot be explained;
— In the circle of love within twin soul, —
And without fear of being cast away,
Or declared unfit for human society...

Could insanity take a heart love's filled?
I feel it couldn't, — for this is as real, —
As sunrise and night in their course' motions,
Ascending and falling in creative cycle.

An intriguing secret's revealing now...
All my past comes to life... true love is found;
And my heart is new — in the love of ours, —
As it cycles our lives in endless bliss!

Love is one of the most misinterpreted emotions. Humans are poorly prepared and instructed on this topic; learning from romance novels, movies and songs that attraction, infatuation and possession is love. We are taken on all the thrilling roller coaster effects of "Love", and lose its essence.

As I sat cerebrating on the word "love", two young girls in their early twenties came by and joined me on my park bench! They were deep in their conversation about a popular novel they had just finished reading.

Listening to their innocent chatter, their expectations; and their ideas of romance, I felt like embracing them — protecting them from the devastating heartbreaking paths — that they were being lured to follow on.

The romance novels groom women into what to dream for and expect from their prince. Society conditions us to believe that the ideal man will sweep us off our feet with gifts and debonair ways. The hero is often — cool but generous to the object of his desire, — and the heroine is blissed to be singled out and to have a courtier to her castle of dreams.

This is called "romance". It does not last and cannot be sustained without stress between both parties. There comes a time when the gifts are not enough to keep the romance alive, — and both start to look elsewhere, or give up completely; continuing their lives together — tied down with responsibilities like diligent robots. They project a false exterior; and unknowingly teach their children that this is how love is supposed to be. The frustration is diffused into society and the result is devastating to all parties concerned.

Love is probably the root for many of the problems in the world today. Instruction on this subject has not been taken seriously; and bad influences flood the youth's minds through media, movies and romantic books.

True Love is the seed of creativity, harmony and kindness. It never generates pain, misery and hurt. It embraces in totality; and spreads grace from two people to the world, diffusing goodness; compassion, warmth and togetherness.

Love suffuses understanding, not only within the blissed couple, but to all they touch in their daily lives, forming the chain of peace.

Choose your life's path, open your heart, spread love to all you meet, day in day out, and the love of your life will find you.

True Love does not fall from trees, it does not drop from the sky, — it does not trick us into the belief — of something that one is instinctively wary of. True Love is soft, it slips into the heart — setting up home as if it had never been away; — and one feels deeply the warmth of its flame.

So, here I sit on my park bench, musing on "Love", and wishing for writers to be fair; to stop using their talents to wallow in possession, infatuation, sadism and masochism; — to raise the level of contents by inspiring hearts and souls, depicting true Love's emotions — when a vision of words that would be said to my love came to me:

"Hello, my love... oh, how I have missed you! My heart has been searching for you... Yes, — it seems to be lifetimes, — but finally I am home now! All has been incomplete without you. The loneliness, the yearning, the nervy pulse in my navel was often so painful, but I never doubted that we would find each other again. I could feel you as you came closer; and somehow I knew that you were nearby!"

"My Love no one will ever be able to separate us again, for we have finally mingled in this life, and our souls can dance, celebrating and witnessing love's sublimity."

Confession of Love

All actions, harmony, justice and wisdom
Can't be hidden, for they are like the tides
Of oceans of life; holy waves of freedom,
Mellific love's gifts that Nature provides!

The creative engine keeps its own speed
Whole, in harmony of synchronization
With Nature's kindness, providing the needs
Complying with its circle of creation...

It is not wise to belittle oneself,
For healthy progressive growth of one's life
Must be showcased on the universe's shelf
As an edifying natural rife!

Many people ask me what is my secret.

— Do I have a secret?

Not a secret, I have a confession: I love myself!

I love my heart and soul, my flesh, my smile, the way my eyes sparkle; my hands when I play the piano, and write of beauty; my voice, the scent of my skin; the feel of my being when I wake in the morning with Helios' smile on my face. The way I walk, my style... yes, love my all...

And it is this love that overflows to you. I wake up each morning wishing to give back, to draw smiles, to touch hearts; to guide souls to fly high and free. Yes, I am wealthy in love and proud of it!

I read my writes over and over, I listen to my recordings as they soothe my soul; and if they soothe me, I know that they are planting seeds of hope and love in all who read and hear them.

So women, love yourselves and the beauty that resides in you! Look at yourselves in the mirror with love, massage your skin and open your hearts to yourselves!

You may ask me: "Don't you think that your words are incredibly egocentric?"

I understand your point. You are influenced by the concept that "everyone knows that to praise oneself is self-centered and conceited." This is an old negative statement of massive brainwash, for to belittle oneself is a weak attitude that will keep one from create wonders and build a prosperous life.

— You have such lovely hair.

"Oh, no... no, this hair is difficult, it goes wild in bad weather!"

— I like your skirt too. It's very like my style.

"This thing? It only cost five dollars."

Listen to yourself! Have you any children?

"Yes, a boy and a girl, twelve and fourteen."

You look so young to have a fourteen year old.

"You wouldn't say that if you were to see me in the mornings!"

— Why don't you love yourself?

"Well, it's just not right. Everyone will criticize and laugh at me."

— Why do you think they would do that?

"I don't know... perhaps because I do that.

There is a lull in the conversation.

— How do you feel when you receive a compliment?

"I feel good, but I instinctively knock myself. I have to admit that when you say you love yourself, it sounds natural. Why is that? What is it about you that ***gives*** you the freedom to be honest? If I behaved as you, I would be called a narcissist!"

I couldn't help but giggle...

Narcissists are dishonest, not only to themselves, but to all around them. The love they have is not real; it is a self defense tool. They feed off enablers like a vampire of the night. Love is an unknown feeling to them, and therefore they do not recognize it. They cause pain whichever way they turn. When one does not truly love oneself, one looks outside for the love so dearly craved, and this kind of love is never enough. More often than not, it is needy, filled with conditions and breeds discontent. Love yourself and be proud. You will be surprised as the world around you changes, your heart opens and soul flies.

"May I tell you a secret?"

Yes.

"I know my hair is lovely, my skirt perfect, and I am beautiful. I just didn't feel that it would be right to admit it."

I could not help but smile as I kissed her on both cheeks and went on my way...

Floating Coffins

An innocent mother, just sixteen,
— Holding a baby to her breast; —
A heart pulsating for relief
Of a situation beyond control,
Boarding a boat to nowhere...
To nowhere or to anywhere...
Grand-mama's money, laces
A hopeful boatman's palm.
Fear and relief, both mingling...
As heart says goodbye to all,
An escaping tear is swiped away...

She knows that her life is balancing
On a cliff of terror, but persevere...
Sitting back, — belongings placed
Tightly between her legs, — eyes closed.
Drawing her baby closer to her...

With her heart pounding she whispers,
"There's only now", and smiles down
On her baby as eyes meet and both
Sleep in an embrace of love and hope.

It is a cold evening, and Sameera draws her baby closer to her chest. This is the only chance she has, she knows it. What a choice... She never imagined this time six months ago that she would — find herself at the mercy — of such a horrific situation. To stay would mean a

life of being raped, and putting her baby girl at risk, to leave now by boat could mean death by starvation, drowning or worse. Her spouse is dead... She tried not to think of the day — the terrorists had come to her village — and killed the father of her baby. She had quickly hidden the baby in her Grand-mama's bed as they burst into her home, raped her... and... She had — promised herself not to think of it again, and leave it all in the past, — but it is so hard to forget...

Yes, she sighed this is her only choice. She boarded the boat. There was a slight sense of hope from the other passengers, although no one dared talk, but she could feel it, just a glimmer. Her baby started to whimper and she quickly fed her breast to the little mouth as their eyes met and she smiled on her little treasure; a smile only a mother can give her baby, a smile of love and care, safety and warmth.

The boatman stood in front of her and she handed him the money her Grand-mama had given her. He took it...

So young, he thought, looking at the child holding her baby.

"Do you have a warm blanket?" He asked.

Sameera nodded affirmatively.

"How about some drink?"

She showed him a bottle of water.

"That's not enough." He said. He made a frantic gesture to his friend. "Hurry! Get her some more water; the baby is going to need it."

After a few minutes he returned with a big bag full of bottles of water.

"Take these and guard them. No matter how desperate the situation, do not give them to anyone. You must take care of yourself first and then your baby. Do you understand?"

She nodded as the boat pulled out to sea.

Sameera said a silent goodbye to her family, her friends and her country. A tear trickled down her cheek. She wiped it from her face annoyed with herself. She did not fear death anymore, but she did fear her baby not having the chance she deserves, a rightful, precious member of the human race.

My heart cries out for the Sameera's of today's world.

Burma is driving the ***Rohingya*** out, many are left with no choice but to board boats in the faint hope for asylum, and allowing themselves to accept the fact that Malaysia,

Thailand and Indonesia will more than likely turn them away. Syrians and Africans are also facing death off the coast of Southern Europe as they flee to escape torture, hunger and traffickers. The world is facing the biggest refugee's crisis since World War II. Governments are allowing them to die in a climate of rising xenophobia! Yes, my heart screams silently as I feel the pain of those turned away again, and I can see the "floating coffins" bodies of lost hope. There are not enough tears in this world to wash away this disgrace!

"Land!" Somebody shouted.

There is a flurry of excitement on the boat. Even Sameera could feel her heart flutter. Her baby is asleep, she is weak. Sameera's breast-milk is drying up, all the water is gone.

A Malaysian boat pulls up beside them and passes out boxes of provisions. Sameera manages to get some water and food for herself and the baby. She feels much relief, and looks around with a faint smile as everyone shares fairly. She can feel so much love, warmth and kindness. While all are eating, talking of their dreams and smiling, they begin to notice that their boat is being pulled back out to sea. A silence falls, like a dark blanket smothering their screams. They all know without words that the unthinkable is happening. There is no anger for they have all been through too much, there are no tears for too many have already been shed and there are no whys, because they have learned from experience that there are no answers.

My heart is burdened with dismay. There is no being on the planet with the right to cause the cruel, slow and inhumane death of another.

Sameera survived all the other passengers. She saw them desperately trying to cling to life; drinking their own urine. She watched her baby girl take her last breath in her arms. And when silence fell and life was no more, she watched her last sun set alone, closed her eyes, and slowed her heart down slipping away from this world... and a deafening scream came through my quill, it shook the Universe as people continued with their lives unaware...

There is power in prayer, when many focus on one hope as souls join and miracles happen. It is at these times that messages from the unknown enter the inner child, solutions are gifted, actions are made, and terror is diffused.

A Lone Warrior

In thoughtful solitude I am with heart steady,
Armor ready — as my soul deeply breathes —
In the atmosphere of courage and sighs...

A nightingale's trying to pull me up:
"Come fly with me", she keeps singing on,
"Leave this human misery." My soul answers,
It's not wise, for many depend on me!

How many more battles do I must face
In life times of blood spill, disgrace and hate?
Oh, Mother Poet, rhyme me with a poem
Whose verses sing Love in stanzas of wonders!

Cherry blossoms shower my reverie
With apologies of scented sweet pleas...
Fuji San hides his noble face behind clouds
Of colorful sunset... as my soul bows
In gratitude for the beauty he beholds;
And the love Japan has bestowed on me.

This country flows through my blood... gently now
With titanic currents of grace in my heart,
As I march forth with courage and wisdom
To announce that only Love is a winner!

Ahmed, a Syrian Angel

Gunshots and explosions are heard nearby
As clouds of fear are blown by winds of terror!
Deep in thought, small hand holding her cloth,
A little boy with his mother, helpless stands.

Helicopter sounds come like a hailstorm.
As people desperately run for shelter,
A thud releases chlorine into the air,
And despaired multitudes scream terrorized.

As one more innocent seraphic life
Pays bills for the craziness of the leaders,
A child whose heart beat for love is dead now.
Mother screams, and the Universe sheds tears.

Who is doing this, the Government, rebels;
— The ICC, (*) UN Security Council,
Cartel of the industrial unrest; —
Or the Lords of this world's programmed wars?

***(*) —* ICC. The International Criminal Court,**
DBA, "International Criminal Cartel."

My Papa is gone. Yes, Mama told me that he had to go to fight for our country. He hugged me tightly before he left, and I saw tears in his eyes. He asked me to take care of Mama. I don't know how I am supposed to take care of Mama; I am only six! Does that mean that Papa isn't coming back?

"Good morning Fatima!"

"Good morning Khaled!"

"Do you want the same as usual?"

"Yes, perhaps a little less rice."

The market place is busy and I am standing beside my Mama. I hear Mama crying every night. She is very quiet, but we have a connection and my chest hurts when she cries. Does Mama's crying mean that Papa isn't coming back? Mama says that Papa is a hero but I hate my country for taking him from us. I think it is hate, I don't really know what hate is. I have heard adults using the word and it seems to mean something that one wants to rid one's life...

"Ahmed!"

I turned to face my mother as I heard the helicopters approaching. Everyone was screaming and running. She caught my hand and we started running from the marketplace towards our house. The ground shook as something dropped behind us.

Mama put her handkerchief against my mouth and we continued running, but suddenly, my legs stopped and I fell to my knees. I couldn't breathe. I felt as if an enormous truck was sitting on my chest. I was gasping for air, but nothing seemed to be getting in. I could see my mother screaming and crying. I was in her arms, and she was still running, but we both knew that it was too late. I could hear voices from every side of the street as we passed, voices laced with terror and screams.

"It's a chlorine bomb!"

"Chlorine... run!"

"Who threw it? Did you see?"

"It was dropped from a helicopter... but no one knows for sure..."

"What does it matter where was it from? The act is inhumane!"

Oh, it hurts so much! Mama! Papa! I cannot hear my voice; no sound seems to be coming out. Now there is a pain in my chest, it is different to the previous heavy feeling, as if my heart is going to explode...

Who is going to take care of Mama? Please don't cry Mama...I don't feel anything anymore. I suddenly felt the air fill my lungs like a crystal glass of water after playing soccer in the street with my friends...

I can suddenly see clearly.

Mama, don't worry, everything will be alright. I said. But no voice came out. I felt her clutching me to her breast. I love you Mama. Her scent is heavenly. I could feel her tears falling on my face as my soul bid this world goodbye.

I found myself in a paradise of peace. There isn't a sound. I must admit that I have forgotten who I am and from where I have come. I feel a tingling all around me and through me. I can feel healing messages...I am no longer a child...I seem to know all. I don't have any sense of time in this paradise, and lie down on soft green grass. How wonderful to breathe, to hear the birds singing, to feel the earth embracing me and see a blue sky above me. I fall asleep...

I wake up smiling. I can hear children's voices and I look behind me. They are playing hide and seek. I joined them. Then, like an incredible whoosh I remember Mama. I must take care of Mama. I know without truly knowing that I can return to see her. I can feel her. I close my eyes and find myself back in our house. Mama is alone. She isn't crying. She is sad, no beyond sad. I know that she cannot see me. I tickle her palm.

"Ahmed, I know you are here, my love. I will be fine. I love you..."

A tear streams down her cheek. I embrace her warmly with my Soul and I see the Light swirl around her and through her. She suddenly stands up and starts gathering ingredients for a meal; and she is smiling and humming to herself.

Then I find myself diving through a tunnel. I can hear Papa's voice. There are gunshots and bombs going off in the background.

"What's up Mohammed? You're very quiet lately."

"I don't know. I just feel that something isn't right."

"It sure isn't! Here we are fighting our brothers. It's a strange and horrendous world."

Papa hasn't heard of my passing on yet...

I knew what I had to do. Yes. I knew without knowing. I will protect Papa until he can return to Mama, and that is what I did for how long, I have no idea. I do not feel time anymore. Papa's friends often commented...

"Mohammed! You live a charmed life!"

Then the day came for him to go home to Mama. I went with him and as they hugged, I returned to the Light.

I feel a pull on my Soul and return to Mama and Papa's house. There is a birthday cake with eleven candles on it, and a little boy and girl about five and three years old.

"Today is Ahmed's birthday. He would have been eleven. When the Syrian uprising took him, he stayed and protected his Mama and I. Without him I would not be alive, and you would not exist. This I believe with all my heart and Soul." Papa said.

"I wish I could see Ahmed..." My little brother said.

"You will sweetheart. When your time comes to pass on from this life, he will be there waiting for you with open arms and that magical smile he always had. Yes, his smile was just like yours." Mama said.

Then she tickled him. My little sister suddenly said: "Happy Birthday Ahmed!"

Then the four of them blow out the candles. I embrace them all tightly with the arms of my Soul. The whole room is filled with Light. Then I go back to where I had come with a sigh of my soul and a smile in my heart, knowing that Time is eternal, — existence is love, — and its light is everywhere.

Calandra and Asli

I woke up in my bed to a beautiful sunny morning. I could hear the children playing in the garden, and the dog whining for a walk. I felt nervous for no obvious reason. I went down to the kitchen for a glass of water. My partner was sitting at the table with his briefcase open shuffling through papers.

Darling?

"Yes..."

Do you believe in other dimensions?

"I have never really thought about it."

Well, do you believe in art?

"Don't be silly!"

What about inspiration?

"What's wrong with you today?"

How about flying through windows of the mind to other places on Earth witnessing happenings?

"I thought you never watch television."

I do sometimes, but this has nothing to do with television.

"Victoria, you are under a lot of stress lately. If you are flying through windows of the mind, you need help."

Really... why?

"Well, you might fly through and never return to your true reality."

Sweetheart, with all your intelligence, you are still living in the past, where people were afraid to talk of such experiences in fear of being locked up; and treated for mental illness.

"Victoria, please talk to someone about all this."

I am talking... to you.

"I mean some professional..."

I had a dream last night...

It should be dawn, but I seem to be sitting on the side of a road at dusk. Did I miss a day? Where am I? I have heard of people getting blackouts, but this is unreal.

I hear a giggle. I look behind a rock and spot a small girl, perhaps ten years old.

What happened to you, Asli? It took ages for you to find me, I nearly fell asleep. We'd better hurry home. Anney will be worried.

I looked into her eyes and noticed that my eyes were on the same level as hers. I slowly began to realize that I am also a little girl.

Asli, are you alright? You look like you have seen a ghost! Hurry up!

It has happened again this loss of control of my mind and body. What is happening to me?

Calandra, wait! I shouted as I run after her down the hill to a village. I know her name...

I follow her into the kitchen.

Well girls, it's about time. I was going to look for you.

"Sorry Anney. We were playing hide and seek. It took Asli ages to find me." Calandra explained.

I sat down by the fire, realizing that Calandra and Anney are conversing in Turkish, and I understand everything. "Heavens, it's only a language!" A voice in my mind whispered softly. I knew in a flash that I could converse in any language...

I stood up and began to lay the table. Anney had made bread, yogurt and goat's cheese. We are all very hungry. I suddenly feel dizzy...

"Asli!" Calandra screamed. "Anney, Asli is really strange today."

Anney put her hand on my forehead. "You have a slight temperature, sweetheart; and must go early to bed tonight."

Yes, Anney. I felt so much love for this woman, my mother. I could feel her arms around me, and her soul sweetly singing to mine. I'm fine... truly... I smiled.

"I have good news girls, your father is coming home tomorrow!"

We both smiled widely. Then Grandma came in and sat with us. Calandra is all chat, and everyone is in a blissful mood.

I felt a chill through my body... Come back Asli... come back Asli... a voice whispers through my mind.

"Anney, may I sleep with Asli tonight. We have no school tomorrow."

"Yes, sweetheart."

"Asli, you are very quiet." Grandma suddenly said as she looked deep into my eyes.

"I'm fine, Babaanney."

I looked around our simple house. There was a big rug on the floor and we were now sitting on it. It was a deep red color and had colorful horses, birds and flowers woven through it. I was wearing a long cotton skirt and a headscarf. I had gold bangles on my arms and I could feel earrings dangling as I moved my head. I was slowly becoming aware of this my true reality. Almost like a flash of lightening, I knew every centimeter of this house...yes...my home. I screamed, but no sound came out as I noticed that the family were chatting on regardless.

I had a terrible feeling of foreboding. Something is about to happen and I knew without truly knowing that I must protect Calandra.

"Alright girls, it is time for bed. Come here, give me a kiss." Anney said, her arms wide open as both girls ran into her embrace.

I kissed her on the cheek and threw my arms around her neck. I didn't want to let go... I felt that I shouldn't, mustn't let go.

"What a lovely hug darling, now off to bed." Anney said.

I went over to Grandma and hugged her.

"Goodnight Asli sweetheart. See you in the morning. Let's make some fresh goat's cheese for your father."

"Yes and sweets, lots of sweets." Calandra said.

Within a few minutes all was silent. I turned to my side and looked at Calandra. She looked peaceful and I could see a slight smile. I seemed to lie awake forever. And then I felt it, so faint, yet I knew.

"Calandra, Calandra wake up! Come with me..."

I pulled her from the bed and told her to wait under the table. Then I ran to my mother's bed and whispered.

"Anney, Anney! Please get under the table with Calandra."

Suddenly, a strong vibration rocked the earth. I ran to Grandma's bed, and dragged her to the table as the roof fell and all went dark.

"Alright, Victoria... the news is about to start. If there is something about your dream in this, perhaps you have some kind of freakish gift. However, if there isn't. Will you stop all this nonsense?"

Victoria silently sat down.

"An earthquake in Turkey has taken thousands of lives..."

It is just a coincidence." He said as he stood up to answer the phone.

The cameraman is walking through an area of survivors, and stops by an old woman, young woman and child.

Calandra... I whispered.

"Yes, we are lucky to have survived. So many of our neighbors are dead..." Anney explained.

Calandra looked in shock. Then her face brightens up as she hears a voice shouting.

"Calandra! Look... I found some bread."

"This is my other daughter, Asli, she saved our lives...she felt the first tremor before us and managed to wake us up and get us safely under a table. Strangely though, she doesn't remember anything."

I picked up the remote, and switched off the television. Then, I closed my eyes and embraced Asli, Calandra, Anney and Babaanney with the arms of my soul; and whispered... "See, miracles do happen."

Alexei's Survival

"Hello, my Love, where have you been? I haven't seen you in two days."

— Where am I? This is becoming more than any joke to bear. — Who is this man addressing me with such familiarity? I look down at my hand. There is a key in it... a key I just let myself into this apartment with. I feel a flush of heat throughout my body and a sudden chill as I realize that I have moved bodies again.

Alexei, just a minute, I need to freshen up.

— "What do you mean by 'freshen up'? You disappear for two days, and come back with an 'I need to freshen up'! I have been worried to distraction."

He is speaking Russian.

Sweetheart, I will be back in a minute.

I rushed through the bedroom to the bathroom, and stopped when I caught sight of my reflection in the mirror. The face that met me was unfamiliar. I touched my cheek, and with a whoosh I knew everything. I could hear gunfire in the background, and I kept thinking of Elena.

— Who is Elena?

"You are Elena, silly!" A voice whispered in my head.

I suddenly understood that something was about to happen...

I walked back to the living room.

"How many times do I have to tell you, my Love? Times have changed. You cannot keep disappearing for underground stories. I worry myself sick!"

I walked into the kitchen for a glass of water. I could feel this strong vibration all around me, and I felt queasy. Alexei had a glass of whiskey in his hand, and was looking out the window. I suddenly felt a surge of energy as all of my senses became acute.

Alexei! I screamed as I lunged towards him, knocking him to the floor just as a bullet swished through the apartment into the wall. Then all went dark.

"You know you shouldn't be traveling like this. You were born under Saturn, and you are defying my rule. You are only one being. I am all powerful. Anything you try in this lifetime, no matter your gifts, will be sabotaged. I always win!"

I smiled, I couldn't help myself. I have never expected life to be easy.

To touch me on Earth is easy; however I cannot be touched here. We both know this. I am not alone anymore... Then a sweet voice said, "Forget this dream..."

I awoke to my Love's embrace, and Helios kissing my face. I smiled and sat up on the bed. I did not turn on the television this time, as I know without knowing that a prominent Russian politician had been saved from assassination. I also know that he will bring wondrous change to world affairs.

However, I am intrigued with Saturn, and decided to research more, for I often feel as if there is an invisible conspiracy against many great people who suffer unnecessarily in this life, only to leave a legacy of Wisdom, Beauty and Truth behind!

Perhaps they know that life is fleeting, and fear has no role in creativity. Yes, that to the outsider their lives may seem cruel, but to each and every one of them, all small blissful creative and inspiring moments erase any discomfort, and embrace their souls with warmth of sincerity that many never touch.

Sunset Reverie

Helios, your light's moving away,
It is dimming very fast now...
Could you hold it a little longer?
— My mother is proud of my schedule,
My chariot follows its timing!

Sitting on a rock, an audience
To the splendor of the sunset;
A challenging day peaceful leaving,
Rewards me with a beauteous site,
Like a paean to Mother Nature!

Perfection abounds; enchants me...
Inspiration refills my heart!
My soul is courageously dancing
To love, gratitude; peace and justice,
Before the twilight and dusk come.

I started my day on an out of control track! The disarray reigned, and all seemed to go wrong. I screamed to the heavens, for my routine was disturbed, and the unexpected occurred, albeit I can smile now; — as my narrow track for the day had led me to be here — viewing this wonderful farewell of the day!

I am sitting on a rock overlooking the ocean, and enjoying a sunset fit for the eyes of the Olympians... It is a poem of Mother Nature witnessing her Majesty! Thank you world, thank you time — for placing me here — to show me reasons to live for, enriching my soul with beauty and charm; — and strength to protect all those who need me, — and to love with my heart and soul.

How diligently we humans try to perfect our surroundings, — making our houses just so, our figures just so, our actions calculated just so; — much stress invited into our lives to climb to new levels of our idea of perfection. Then one takes a break and walks outside into Nature's realms, where all fits in perfect harmony: trees branch out in different directions; flowers color the world, birds sing their tunes, and the sunset, — that I am now feasting my eyes with — on whispering to me of peace and hope; wisdom and courage, love and growth.

Helios blinked his farewell; — another day fades away — making a path for tomorrow... I will sleep well tonight, for I will dream of you; and you, and you...

Jinmenju

Momiji attached his wooden sword to his belt and ran downstairs to the kitchen. There was an aroma of freshly baked pound cake.

"Mama, I have a mission. I will need to bring some food with me."

Hinako looked at her ten year old son. He was certainly dressed for an adventure with his samurai sword and headband. She knew that this was indeed a serious day!

"Alright, I will make you some onigiris for your journey. Would you like some oranges too?"

"I don't need oranges as I am going to find the Jinmenju, and I shall eat its fruit."

"Understood!" said Hinako. "Please be careful and don't be late for dinner."

Momiji looked up. "What's for dinner, Mama?"

"Curry rice", she said as she busied herself around the kitchen.

"Well, I'm off." He said, putting on a small backpack. He walked out onto the porch. His grandma was sitting outside pealing radishes.

"Bye grandma, see you later, I am going to find the Jinmenju."

"Momiji, please be careful of the Jubokko!"

"The what?"

Momiji came to a halt and swung around.

"The Jubokko." Grandma said as she dried her hands on a towel hanging from her waist.

"It is an extremely deceptive tree. From a distance it looks innocent, however if you look closely enough, you will see that the branches could grab you and the base of the tree resembles piled up human remains. When you see it, I suggest that you run away before you become its next victim!"

"Alright, grandma! I'll be careful." Momiji said as he adjusted his sword.

"Jubokko trees..." Grandma continued, "were normal trees once upon a time, however one day the land they lived on was soaked in blood. When the trees roots absorbed the blood they turned into evil spirit vampire trees, and can now only live off blood. If you get too close, they will grab you and drink all that red liquid inside you. Your body will be left there as food for birds of prey, and your bones will become a part of the tree. So, Momiji... be careful!"

"Yes, Grandma I will be back soon."

"Don't forget that today is curry rice day!"

Grandma watched her grandson, a little ball of light, as he disappeared into the forest. Then she continued to peal the radishes.

Momiji was now alone, just him and the dreaded Jubokko trees! He will stay well clear of them and if they try to snatch him, he will chop of their branches with his trusty sword. He didn't have much time. He needed to reach the Jinmenju before dinner time. Grandma is a fountain of knowledge, he thought. It was she who had brought his attention to the Jinmenju too! This was not his first time to go in search of the Jinmenju, however it was his first time to hear of the Jubokko, and even though he did not show any emotion to his grandma, her story had left him feeling quite nervous. He had no wish to have his blood drained by a vampire tree. As he walked through the thick forest, all the trees seemed to resemble the Jubokko. By and by, he came to a stream. He removed his sandals and sat on a rock placing his feet into the clear water. Then he started eating his onigiri quietly being pulled into the serenity of this magical place. Suddenly he felt something nudging his feet. He looked down to see a huge orange carp looking up at him with mouth open.

"Hello!" Momiji said. "You gave me quite a fright."

"Hello Momiji!" said the carp.

"How do you know my name?" Momiji asked, trying to keep the astonishment out of his voice.

"I know everything." The carp boasted.

"Well then, perhaps you can tell me where I can find the Jinmenju."

"I can and I will if you give me some of that delicious onigiri."

"Certainly!" Said Momiji as he placed some morsels of rice into the carp's mouth.

"Thank you, Momiji! The Jinmenju is on top of that hill, however you have to pass a few Jubokkos so be very careful!"

"I will!" Momiji said, as he packed up, dried his feet with a small hand towel and put on his sandals.

The carp swam away...

Momiji had hardly been walking five minutes when he

saw the first Jubokko. The tree seemed to smile at him, and to Momiji's eyes it looked beautiful, although he was aware that he was being lured into its warm embrace.

Almost in a trance, he walked closer to the tree, and then he heard his grandma's voice in his head: "Momiji! It's a trap. Take your eyes off the tree!"

He immediately awoke and returned to the path avoiding any kind of eye contact with the magnificent tree! He passed a few more and each time his grandma warned him. "How did she know where he is?" He thought feeling puzzled.

Then he saw it... the Jinmenju standing gloriously, its branches filled with fruit. Momiji's mouth dropped open, it was just as he had heard; the fruit resembled human faces. He knew that if he passed the tree, the fruit would laugh, probably scare him into a run; and he would never be able to find the tree again. So Momiji stood his ground. To conquer this fear there was something he would have to do. He opened his mouth and started laughing. The more he laughed, the more fruit fell from the tree. He picked up a piece and bit into it. It tasted just as grandma had said, like an orange. Then he put one into his backpack and headed home. The Jubokko trees had disappeared and he knew that by eating the fruit, he had become a true life warrior.

He returned just in time for dinner. Grandma was tidying up and she smiled to see him home safe and sound.

"Grandma, how did you know that I was near a Jubokko?"

"Well, I could see you." She said. "You are a little ball of light; there is no hiding for you."

"I brought you a present." Momiji said. "If you eat this fruit, you will be a life warrior like me."

"Thank you, sweetheart." She said, as a tear trickled down her cheek. Then they heard Momiji's mother calling them to the dining room, and they both went inside as a full moon shone down on the wonder of Love.

Kuchisake Onna

Momiji's mother sounded concerned.

"Grandma, is Momiji home yet?"

"Don't worry, he will be back soon." Grandma assured her.

"Well, he is now at the magical age of ten and able to walk home from school alone. However, lately the days are shorter. The sky is heavy with snow and the sun has already set."

"What's for dinner?" Grandma asked.

Momiji's mother laughed, and said: "Tempura, miso soup pickles and rice."

"They sound delicious." Grandma replied. She is sitting at the kotatsu folding the laundry. "I hope Momiji remembers to watch out for the Kuchisake Onna, and finds the sweeties I put in his jacket pocket." She thought.

Momiji is still twenty minutes from home. He had been playing soccer with his friends in the school playground. Usually there is a rule to return home once before playing, but as the day is so short he had hid his school bag behind a wall and was only now returning. Mama will be angry, he thought. He didn't realize how late it became. Now the path home is dark and lonely. He starts humming a tune as he kicks a stone ahead of him. He played well today, three goals! Momiji smiles widely. When he grows up, he is going to be a professional soccer player. His hands are getting cold so he places them in his jacket pocket. He feels some sweets and starts toying with them. Suddenly he realizes their purpose and quietly raises his head. Now on alert, he is no longer the small boy on his way home from school, he is Momiji the Life Warrior.

Grandma had put the sweets in his pocket to protect him from Kuchisake Onna. "She is a woman wearing a surgical mask who appears before children walking alone at night." Momiji knows what to do. Does Momiji believe in her? Of course he does, and he is ready. All the sweets in his pocket are being grasped tightly in his little fist. A cold breeze makes him shudder... and then he sees her waiting for him at the top of the hill. He could avoid her by making a long detour, but that would not be his style. He does not change his pace and keeps his back straight; head up and heart steady. He decides that he will not look into her eyes as that would surely be an image to haunt him forever. As he approaches, the woman does not move. He is about to pass her when she says...

"Am I pretty?"

Momiji shudders, he is speechless. Then he hears grandma's voice in his head telling him what to say.

"Yes." He answered for he knew that if he said no she would stab him to death with a scissors she always carries.

Then she removes her mask. Momiji is very careful to keep his gaze on her mouth. It is slit from ear to ear just as grandma had said. The Kuchisake Onna had been mutilated by her husband and is now a malicious spirit.

"And how about now, what do think?"

Momiji knows that if he says... no... and runs she will appear in front of him and kill him. If he says yes... she will still kill him. Grandma said there is only one way. He must confuse her.

"You are average, so, so". He answered.

As she is unsure of what to do, Momiji is given time to run. When she becomes aware of him getting away, he throws a fistful of sweets. She stops to pick them up and he runs non-stop all the way home. Grandma is on the porch waiting for him as she has seen his little light.

"Grandma, I met the Kuchisake Onna!"

"And you survived, I see."

"Yes!" Momiji answered proudly.

Then Mama came outside.

"Momiji! You are so late. What did I tell you about playing soccer after school? You must come home earlier during the winter months."

"Yes, Mama, I'm sorry. Would you like a sweet?"

"Thank you, cheeky! Go in and wash your hands. Dinner is ready."

"Mama, you are beautiful!"

"What's got into you?" Mama giggled. "You're beautiful too! Come on grandma, let's eat!"

"I am coming now." Grandma said, looking off into the distance as she could see the Kuchisake Onna disappearing into the night sky as snow began to fall, and nature took its lovely course...

In Despair

There is only so much a mind can take when despair visits, and all other emotions are thrown into a tizzy.

"What happened to you today? Why are you sitting here in this lifeless room surrounded by four handmade walls depending on the narrowness of humanity to you from devastation?"

My sudden silence filled the room as my entrance had been like an earthquake.

The dawn is here, I thought, as light entered my darkness. I had sat up all night wondering in despair. I have never felt so out of control; — spiraling down into a dark hole — void of love and caring. I am so alone, so utterly, devastatingly lonely. I am loved by many, but not enough.

How I dream to be wrapped in warmth and to release all my burdens for sixty seconds. Yes, this is desperation, and I am living it. My eyes are heavy, swollen and sore, I feel like vomiting; — wanting to rid myself of my very guts, — but nothing comes out from my empty stomach. There is no relief.

I can see dark smoke enveloping me, but I don't have the energy and will power to get rid of it. My whole being screams for help, but no sound passes my still lips.

The children woke up earlier. I must not show them this miserable me. I was bright, smiley, kissing and cuddling them before I sent them off to school; and then I fell back into this loneliness of my soul.

I hide here not wanting to meet anyone. Voices pierce my ears painfully, intrusive questions irritate me, and so I have become alone and introverted. This is the longest bout of misery I have ever felt. I question my sanity and wonder why the sun of my world refuses to rise again. I am so ashamed of my weakness!

When despair creeps in after all other avenues have failed in one's mind. We hear our silent scream to the cosmos, asking the reason for it to be taking our peace.

"This emotion is not real, it is a trick; an illusion of the mind. There is a cure for it, so simple it can draw giggles," said my inner voice, and suggested: "Drink some water, open the door, and walk out of your man made 'paradise', and back into the warm, loving embrace of Life; synchronizing wonders to value the treasure of your existence now, walking proud as a blissed human being!"

Butterfly

I was sitting peacefully by a pond,
She came fluttering into my dawn
Landing on my stillness gently...
"Come fly with me..." she whispered.
Willing, without doubt I adhered.

We flew through fields of sunflowers,
— All smiling in sublime homage
To Nature in reverent radiance; —
Colorful skies with hues of rainbows...

I smiled, giggled and chatted nonstop,
Until silence reigned in my heart;
And her love alimented my soul.
We returned to the peaceful pond,
Diffusing scents and kissing flowers.

When we landed, I looked at her beauty,
And serenely with a grateful heart
I thanked her for the magical dawn.

Papilio's Caress

The caress' power of a butterfly
Diffuses its energy through me,
And love flows mellifluously to meet
A glorious day of gentle promises...
Opening my eyes to the rhythm of life,
I listen heedfully to Nature wise voice;
Sensing its truth that embraces my soul,
As the universe of harmony flows!

I hear you, — like auscultating your heart —
I breathe life cherishing all of my being
Now to live to care, caring to exist
In peace, as quality learning and sharing
— Become a reality of daily smiles —
Of wonders to a courageous open heart.

It had been a busy Helios day, hence a slow Monday morning as I tried to get three reluctant children to school. My ankle was throbbing, but in all honesty, it was not so bad. I have had worse sprained ankles in my lifetime. Yesterday, I had stumbled on my heels, and this morning I am paying the price of a careless second.

How beautiful Selene had been last night, and now I was blessed with Helios' smile. Birds are singing, children giggling and a new born baby is crying next door.

I open all the windows, and as I prepare the breakfast, I listen to the magical sound of a new existence crying for attention, understanding and a sweet life.

Billy, Alex! Hurry up! It's time to go. Did you brush your teeth? Put on your shoes, caps, schoolbags... bye... wait... kisses... hugs...

"Mama, we're going to be late!" Alex smiled.

See you soon, sweethearts... be good!

"Mama, I love you!" Billy screamed from the gate as he and Alex, both burst into a run to catch up with their friends.

Bella is lying on the sofa with a blanket over her.

"Mama, I have a headache. I can't possibly go now."

Alright, I will call the school and tell them.

"I will be fine in an hour or so..." She said.

I started tidying away the dishes when Joey, our dog, let an indignant holler.

Bella, I am going to take Joey for a walk.

"You shouldn't Mama; you need to rest your foot."

I know sweetheart, but listen to him.

I got a bag for his poop, and he could sense exactly what I am up to as he started jumping around excitedly in anticipation of my arrival. I put the lead on him and half limped to the park, then I freed him, and he ran off into the mountains, tail held high, and a wide smile on his snout and a dance of a run. He stopped to christen a bush, lifting his legs up high into a front paw stand and I couldn't help but smile, for all I could see was a little ball of light.

I walked to a tree in the park where I had seen Joey poop and picked it up with the bag; and then, as I straightened up, — a beautiful blue butterfly — landed on my sore foot. I looked down on a little being, and felt blissed. It stayed there for quite some time gifting me with its beauty, serenity, and bringing stillness to my morning with a wave of warmth. Just as Joey returned, it flew away. Joey stood smiling before me... Well, let's go... I said.

I put the lead on him, and returned home. Within a couple of hours, my foot was healed.

To be aware enough to feel the love from a butterfly is indeed a gift from the universe. The Poet who exists ninety-nine percent throughout my being whispers... believe... and of course I do.

A Trip Home

The night is still as dark as soot,
Scent is felt as feet move forward.
Ana steps onto a path she knows well...
Suddenly stargazers light up
Under the moon in full bloom!

Magnolia Lass appears nearby,
Eyes sparkling blissed healthy smiles;
Familiar faces join the walk,
And soon they reached a clearing.

Everyone stands facing Ana,
As the leader walks towards her;
Her eyes drink in each one of them,
Pain subsides as the still embraces.

With arms opened wide she smiles,
It's time to move on... she cries...
Her heart opens as all absorb into her.

Now silent except for the leader's box
Filled with the jewels of her lives...
When she opens it, a rainbow of colors
Appears in the skies; and smiling, Ana
Takes safe flight into a new Light.

Ana finds herself on that familiar path, Supreme by her side. Stargazers lined up sparkling under Selene's kiss in full bloom. Her eyes become accustomed to the darkness, she sees Magnolia Lass approaching, her beautiful eyes looking deeply into Ana's all-knowing yet not wanting to move on.

This journey has come to a close, sweet Magnolia.

As Ana reaches the clearing, all is waiting. There is no violin playing, no fire, no laughter, no tears, no happiness, no sadness, just stillness. The leader smiles.

"Thank you," Ana said, "I love all of you!"

There is no emotion, just acceptance, peace and readiness. Ana opens her arms wide. "Let's move on!" She cried.

All her dear friends absorb into her, except the leader. He stands in front of her holding his treasured box filled with the jewels of her lives. A tear trickles as their eyes meet.

"You did it, Ana." He whispered.

"We did it. Thank you... Come. It is time to go..."

"Wait! Don't forget me!"

They turned to see Piedri walking swiftly towards them. He has a very special rose in his hand.

"This is for Usianus." He said with a smile.

The leader places the box in the center, and they join

hands around it as it opens shooting a rainbow of colors.They take flight through skies of Love, Light, Courage, Wisdom and Peace. And then they see it, their beautiful planet of Usianus waiting patiently for their return.

Ana releases all the souls and they dance around. Dimitri plays his violin, Piedri caresses the flowers with his eyes, stooping down to plant his prize, Crystalia breaths in the fresh air, Alex runs after the butterflies, the leader embraces his true love who had been waiting always invisibly by his side, and Sunaisu stands by the river; arms opened wide as Ana runs into his loving embrace.

"Welcome back, my Usian." He said, and she suddenly loses all her strength. It was such a long journey.

"Sunaisu, I was and am always with you."

"I know, my Love."

Some children run up to Usian, she hugs them tightly.

"Usian." Said Meara, a six year old child with sparkling eyes. "Please don't go back, stay here."

"Sweetheart, I am never gone long. My darling, this is how we fight our battles. We infiltrate and try to conquer with Love. I must go back. I have very strong soul connections. I need to guide them."

"I know Usian, it's just that we miss you so much. The whole planet misses you, and sometimes Sunaisu is gone too!"

"Yes, but we are never truly gone Meara. It just seems

that way, and we always return. When you grow up, you will have to go too. Usianus will be proud of the warrior you will become!"

"I want to be just like you, Usian!"

"Emmanuelle has organized a huge banquet. A few other missions also returned this evening. It is a glorious day for Usianus. We have musicians, poets, actors and artists all ready to participate!"

"Well, I will just go home to freshen up. Then let's play!"

Usian places her hand in Sunaisu's and they start walking to the house.

"Oh, my Love, look at the Selene's twin this evening. They are so beautiful."

He silently squeezes her hand. She can feel the release of worry within him, the Love, and the wanting.

"Us is Us forever, my Precious..." She whispered.

"It was good to be home..."

There was a sound of a door opening...

Ana looked up to see the Child Welfare officer.

"We have finished talking to the children. Thank you!"

"Mama!Mama!"

Ana opened her arms as the children ran into her embrace.

"May we eat out tonight?"

"Of course my love, she said all smiles."

"Mama, what were you doing?"

Just scribbling

"Show us!"

Ana showed her notebook where a beautifully sketched rose smiled back. Then they all held hands and strolled out of the courthouse.

Violence

Observing facts and actions through their mind's eye,
Vincent Van Gogh and Francis Bacon, peeled
The innocent exterior off the subject studied,
Depicting the violence inside of each...

We are ravaged, although we strive for beauty,
Innocence; and peace as we are all addicted
To the lull... the hush... the silence... the after...

Violence is reigning in each blade of grass;
In the slewing of an insect by another;
In the appearance of weeds; in a stormy
Day as nature rants and raves with typhoons,
Hurricanes, deluge; and earthquakes!

We too, are born into violence, and live
To practice it; and tolerate it cowardly!

Most of the atrocities on Earth were,
And are practiced under the orders,
And or by consent of religious leaders;
All chronicled in the journals of history
In the library of shame and immorality!

The Notes between the Notes

Notes fall from the sky in my heart...
Unheard songs singing true love's grace;
A master plays to please my soul
With his violin of enchantment.

Dimi's touching — my being holds
With sublime energy of wonders.
Holding hands, listening to songs
Of beauty... magic time of love!

A mingling of caressing's balm,
Healing power dives through my veins;
Gratitude I sigh, and inhale
Air of the atmosphere of joy!

I walk through a wood towards a beauteous sound. The sun has just risen, and earth is vibrating with life's energy. I see him standing in a clearing, playing his violin. His familiar stance so endearing... I sneak up behind him covering his eyes with my hands.

"Ana!" — He screams swinging around: "My soul told me you were coming."

"Dimi ... You called me... You knew I would come!"

"Of course I knew..." He said as he lifts me twirling around, and around, until we both fall onto the soft grass;

laughing, remembering that feeling, that scent of wondrous times long past. Lying on our backs looking up at the clear morning sky, Dimi grasps my hand and we both turn our heads to drink in smiles."

"How did you know it was me?"

"That's easy, your step, your heartbeat and your rose's fragrance."

"Ana, do you remember our music, — the notes between the notes, — the ones that can only be heard by few?"

Yes, I do, and I still hear them singing in my heart, when loneliness visits. I hear them in the raindrops, in the flutter of butterfly's wings; in the beauty of a sunset, in a full moon; and in a gentle breeze, a trickling stream; and I hear them as a flower blooms opening each petal, one by one; and each petal differently. Dimi, I hear them riding my soul when your heart whispers to me. I hear them sweet Dimi, always... and I listen to them.

"I often play them for you."

"Yes, they vibrate right through me and I awake blissed."

I sat up looking down on Dimi's face. He looked so happy. His green eyes were dancing mischievously.

Look at you! You haven't changed a bit. You would love to start teasing me, wouldn't you?

"You have always been teasable!"

I silently lay back again, and then my inner voice said: "Oh, Ana, he is suffering so. Please go to him, talk to him..."

Lately his heart aches. I am hearing the notes, the ones he hides from others.

A tear trickles down my cheek, for my chest hurts. Dimi squeezes my hand.

"Don't worry, Ana, he is strong, a great leader with a victorious heart!" I heard my inner voice again.

I know Dimi, but I feel his pain...

"It is time for us to go our separate ways... see you soon... my precious Ana."

Silence falls slowly as Dimi's beautiful music fades into the distance. I sit up clutching my chest as tears trickle down my cheeks, take a deep breath and start walking back the way I had come.

"Ana! Please, come to me, sleep with me a little, let me just put my arms around you and hold you close. Honored I am, my Love!" The pain on my chest intensifies...

"Mama, you will catch a cold!"

I opened my eyes to see my daughter gazing down on me as I lay in the garden with pen and paper resting on my chest.

Thank you, my Love; I am coming in now...

A Dream in a Dream

A Dream in a dream of eternal souls,
In transcendental imagery and feelings;
An incontestable fact lived, — proved —
To satisfy me in my will to freedom.

I can feel his presence in any form;
In the fragrance formula of lime oil,
And the essence of cinnamon combined,
For our souls have codes to reunite us.

We have found each other in many bodies,
— Anatomy of bio existence; —
In all secular and artistic functions
That our eternal energy may flow.

Strawberry was a key to our romance...
Returning from military campaigns,
He enjoyed to toast our love with vintage
Wine, never missing a fine champagne!

My eyes rose to see the chandelier. How could I know each crystal so intimately, as if I had lain in this hall looking up at them for hours? I was sitting on an X-chair, dressed in blue with white lace; and as my eyes rested on my white gloved hands, I noticed a card. So this is a dance card, I thought briefly. I opened it to look inside... A fragrance of lime mingled with cinnamon I felt... There was only one name repeated over and over again. I found myself smiling, as to why, I have no idea, but I must say that my heart was all a flutter at just the simple sight of his name. I suddenly wished I could take a look at myself in a mirror. What do I look like? I wondered as the music started up. There were groups of people standing around, chatting and I seemed to know no one.

"Claudia, you are very distant tonight, aren't you feeling well?"

I turned to my right; a familiar face was looking at me concerned. I knew knew her but didn't know her.

"Would you like to go upstairs to lie down for a while?"

So, this magnificent house is where I live. How wondrous, I thought as I turned to smile assuring her that I am fine.

"He will be here soon, sweetheart, don't worry. He came back safely. Actually he seems to lead a charmed life. I have no idea as to how he avoids injuries through so many battles."

I smile silently as I scanned the ball room. When I turned my gaze to my left, my eyes met in a mirror. My face was as it has been and I smiled on recognition. A thousand questions flooded my mind, and a beautiful voice inside my head, whispered: "Shhh... Ana... after this."

Yes, Ana, not Claudia.

"Hello Beauty!"

I raised my eyes to see him. His handsome face unchanged through lifetimes, his eyes looking into mine, creating the same magical effect of yore. He took my hand and led me to the dance floor, pulling me close to him as my soul dived into his. I could feel his breath and heartbeat, his heavenly scent; and dancing was the last thought in my mind as it swirled through passions lanes and love's dreams. We did not move our gaze from one to one. I wanted to talk, but not a word could I utter.

Oh, my love, it is wonderful to feel you in the flesh! I wake up each morning to your kisses and caresses, my precious and I feel grateful for us, but I do yearn to be with you in body all the time.

"Well, here we are!" he said with a wide smile as we swirled around the dance floor.

I listened to his entertaining stories of his travels and he listened to the wanderings of my mind as we drank in our essence with insatiable thirst.

Then suddenly all went black, my hands groping for something familiar. He was gone!

Where am I? I asked myself... I had this terrible feeling of dread in my chest. Suddenly I realized that I was flying through a dark tunnel at great speed.

"Ana! Ana!"

He was calling me; I had to get to him now. No... now is not fast enough! I relaxed into the journey as my heart attempted to scream, fear embracing within. Then I was blinded by light as I found myself hovering over the battlefield. My eyes scanned the bloody carnage for my love. I could hear him calling my name, and my soul found him leaning against a rock, a knife through his chest, his eyes unfocused and breath shallow.

I am here, my love, I whispered to his heart.

I swirled around him feverishly trying to save him, heal him; keep him here in this life with me, but to no avail. I caught him as he slid from the rock, and laid his head in my lap, stroking his hair as tears streamed from every pore of my being.

It's alright, my love, I am here with you... I whispered.

His face lit up momentarily as our eyes met... "Ana, I am always near you, and I will find you in every lifetime!" Were his last words as my heart cried out painfully; and then he left his body... I screamed silently to the heavens.

I awoke in my bed. My pillow and sheets wet with tears. There were many knocks on the door, and then a woman entered, that was my mother...

"Darling, I have some bad news..."

I am fine, Mama, please let me be alone for a while. I responded.

She left the room quietly, and I sat on the bed, staring at the wall across from me. Then I felt his kiss, I felt his caress, I heard his words ever so silently.

"Ana, I love you for all eternity."

I stood up and went by the window to take a look down on the garden. It was spring, and the world was living on. The sun shone on my face, and I felt my love's arms embracing me...

"Wake up, darling, let's take a walk."

Oh, my love, I had such an incredible dream. It was about the transmigration of souls; a reality that can be confirmed in many ways, inclusive in biochemistry. It won't be long for the "DNA" of the souls to be proved scientifically, as cloning is today; and that might be the knowledge required to unite the Human Race.

I was back home, in my time, in the present, the now of my soul, and he was with me, yes, he was with me again...

"Strawberries?!" he asked with a twinkle. That was his way to mean, "Let's celebrate this moment with champagne!"

Come here you! Who needs strawberries?! I said as he cuddled back into bed with me.

Insistent knocks on the door woke me up again... My mother entered...

"Darling, get up and come for breakfast, I made cinnamon rolls today; have fresh flowers on the table, and a tray filled with strawberries..."

"The Leader"

Piedri's newly painted caravan glow
Under the glorious smile of Selene
A candlelit inside invites me in...
There, he is sipping wine, looking forlorn.

Not lives visited in his sweet embrace,
Unshed tears are held in with quiet grace;
Magical thoughts of a daisy chain's bliss;
Kicking stones of grief on the path of sorrow.

One may have blunders, but all can be right
With creative actions of true beliefs,
And perseverance of love's attitude
Steady as a nightingale's holy song!

It was night as I became aware of my certain step's sound, direction; and determination. Piedri's beautifully painted caravan was lit up by the moon. All was calm as I took a deep breath, and reached the door; ajar most of the time, but now closed. I could see candlelight through the window, and I knew that he was still up, knowing that I was about to arrive. I opened the door, and walked in quietly. He was there sitting at a round table drinking wine.

"Have some wine, Ana." He said gently. I sat down beside him without answering; and asked: "Why do you keep calling me, sweetheart?"

"My soul calls you all the time, Ana, so naturally."

Then he smiles into my eyes. He always had a twinkle, a tiny bit of mischief, when he looked at me, and my eyes automatically shot stars into his, for this is the way we have always been.

"I can't sleep. I have been waiting for you..."

"I don't think you should be drinking wine if you are sick."

I smile, how well I know this man, the leader of my people; strong, courageous and true; a heart big enough to embrace the world. Such power he possesses! He is a part of my soul, there is no denying it; and to sit beside him even for such a short while is bliss itself. I knew he felt the same way about me, for our past and present existence can never be questioned.

"Ana, please sleep with me and rub my tummy."

Sleep with you? I believe that would be difficult as one thing would probably lead to another!

A flash of anger crossed his handsome face. I knew at that moment that I could have kissed him one way to the heavens!

"How could you even think that I would...?"

I suddenly felt sad, an overwhelming painful grip in my chest.

I will lie with you sweetheart...

He lay down on the bed, and I rested my head on his chest as he held me close. My hand made circular motions on his tummy, releasing all the bad energy. I could feel him tighten his embrace and smell my hair as my body molded into his and I dozed off.

We were walking hand in hand through a forest, so young, I was sixteen. It was first love, the first love of all our existences. Sunlight was casting shadows through the trees; birds were singing brightly, yes, it was spring. We talked peaceful and cheerfully, teasing each other and smiling. All was blissful! I realized that I was holding the leader's hand and we were looking down on our young forms from above.

"Ana, will you love me forever?"

"Of course I will, silly! What a question!"

Ana was now sitting on the lawn making a daisy chain. He was kicking stones around, walking with hands in his pockets.

"Ana, if you leave me, I will spend many lives searching for you!"

Honey, you are breaking my heart. I will never leave you. Come here and sit down.

I woke up in his arms. He was sleeping soundly, his tummy now healed. I did not want to leave his embrace, but I knew that I had to, for a lot had happened since then, a lot of wrongs that had to be put right. I closed my eyes inhaling his scent, slipped quietly from his embrace and walked to the door.

"Thank you Ana, I love you!" He murmured.

I felt a stab in my chest as I walked back along the track to my "reality."

Spring sunshine warmed me from my slumber. I was hugging my pillow with all my might. I could hear birds singing, and I pulled myself from bed just as my phone rang out.